PENIS PUNS

PENIS PUNS

A Movie Quote Book

Compiled & Edited
By Steve Stewart

COMPANION
★ P ★ R ★ E ★ S ★ S

Copyright © 1997 by Steve Stewart

COMPANION PRESS
PO Box 2575, Laguna Hills, California 92654

PRINTED IN CANADA
First Printing 1997

ISBN: 1-889138-07-X

This book is dedicated to all the put-down penises of the world—
may they once again stand tall and proud!

ACKNOWLEDGMENTS

I'd like to thank all of the individuals who, in one way or another, contributed to this book by suggesting that I see movies that I might not otherwise have seen.

They include: Harold Blumenfeld, Wayne Brean, Charles Cook, Bill Daniels, Charles Dearnley, Steve Desjardins, Michael Ferguson, Steve Finn, Gillian Flynn, Valerie Frazee, Dave Gill, Boze Hadleigh, Troy Hatlevig, Michael Henderson, Dave Hutchinson, Donald Jacobs, Jamoo, Don Lort, Sean Magner, Ray Martin, Claude P. Matundan, Stevan McKie, Paul Montgomerie, F. Michael Moore, R. Munro, James Robert Parish, John Patricks, Lance Perkins, Georgene Rada, Benjamin Russeau, Sabin, Marc Shiflett, Bette Siegel, Jim Simpers, Peggy Stuart, Dan Studer, Brenda Sunoo, Vin Tozzi, Mark Willerton, Keary L. Williams and the hundreds of film buffs from around the world who anonymously have written or e-mailed me with film facts in recent years.

I also would like to thank Aaron Silverman at SCB Distributors for his helpful suggestions and vital support of this book.

Finally, I must thank Jim Fredrickson, once again, for his constant support, advice and encouragement.

INTRODUCTION

"Is that a gun in your pocket, or are you just happy to see me?"
—*Mae West, She Done Him Wrong*

In the opening scene of *Reservoir Dogs* (1992), director and actor Quentin Tarantino explains to Harvey Keitel and Eddie Bunker his theory about the song "Like A Virgin." He says, "It's a metaphor for big dicks … I'm talkin' dick, dick, dick, dick, dick, dick, dick." And so is everyone else these days—especially in the movies.

When Mae West started talking about "it" way back in 1933 she was a pioneer of the penis pun. Her famous double entendre (above) is probably *the* most quoted movie line in film history.

I'm not sure why, but everyone seems to love putting down the penis, berating the boner, insulting the sausage, and well, you get the point. Boobs, butts and occasionally beavers are all put-down on a regular basis in the movies as well, but it's the penis that stands out from the crowd. And most of the barbs are about one thing—size. Of course, blow jobs, masturbation, erections, impotence and premature ejaculation are all part and parcel of penis repartee and dick discourse, but size—no big surprise—comes up for examination more often than any other phallic attribute or activity.

When it isn't being prick teased and ridiculed, it's being nicknamed. There are more euphemisms for the penis than any other body part. Moviemakers have gone to great lengths (pun intended), especially in recent years, to add to the list with ever more clever ways to describe the penis.

In *That Was Then … This Is Now* (1985), Emilio Estevez describes Craig Sheffer's penis as a "one-eyed trouser mouse." Mel Gibson, in *Bird On A Wire* (1990), refers affectionately to his better half as Mr. Wiggly. But in *Four Rooms* (1996), Jennifer Beals tops them both. When David

Proval requests that she "Please stop talking about [another man's] cock!" She replies, "It's hard to stop talking about something so huge! I mean I could go on and on about his cock, his bone, knob, bishop, wang, thang, rod, hot rod, hump mobile, oscar, dong, dagger, banana, sausage, kielbasa, schlong, dick, Big Ben, wee wee, Mr. Happy, Peter, pecker, pee pee, weiner, pisser, pistol, middle leg, third leg, one-eyed wonder, junior, little head, little guy, rumple foreskin, tootsie roll, love muscle, skin mobile, roto rooter, snake ..."

She left out bologna, basket, boner, chubby, cucumber, equipment, hard-on, hose, hot dog, Johnson, lariat, little general, little prince, meat, member, missile, mouse, organ, pee wee, pencil, pickle, prick, rocket, salami, tallywacker, tool, torpedo, willie, woody, worm and quite a few others. But if you watch enough movies they all pop up sooner or later. Many of them in the pages of this book.

Talking about penises in the movies has become so common in the '90s, that quite often it isn't even intended to be funny. It just becomes another topic of conversation. In the comedy *Blue In The Face* (1994), Michael J. Fox asks Giancarlo Esposito, "Are you satisfied with the size and shape of your penis?" Esposito replies, "That's a personal question … No." He then continues, "The length is good, the width is questionable, and I got a little curve to the left." Well, he did ask.

As I've said, everyone is talking about penises in the movies. But not everyone is saying anything you'd want to repeat or quote. This book attempts to be a collection of penis puns, jokes and one-liners that are humorous, stand on their own and are quotable.

So, remember as you turn the page—to paraphrase another popular penis movie pun—"A hard quote is good to find."

Steve Stewart
Laguna Hills, 1997

"I like your movies, man. You've got a great penis."

Val Kilmer
The Doors (1991)

"If a light sleeper can't sleep with a light on, why can a hard sleeper sleep with a hard-on?"

Lin Tucci
Showgirls (1995)

"Honey, Mr. Monkey wants to play."
Stephen Tobolowsky
Dr. Jekyll and Ms. Hyde (1995)

"This is a '70s porno. You know how
I can tell? Cause the guy's dick has
sideburns."

Adam Sandler
Bulletproof (1996)

"Whose butt did you kiss to get in
  here?"
"Well, the list is long, but
  distinguished."
"Yeah, so is my Johnson!"
  Rick Rossovich and Anthony Edwards
  Top Gun (1986)

"Man is not known by inches alone."

Dan Monahan
Porky's (1982)

"Well, my goodness, Scraps is a boy
     dog, isn't he?"
"Yeah."
"Jimmy, do you like it when Scraps
     holds onto your leg and rubs up and
     down?"

> *Peter Graves and Oliver Robins*
> *Airplane II—The Sequel* (1982)

"I'm a total failure."
"Richard, if you're a total failure, why
   do I want to marry you?"
"Because I'm hung like a rhino!"
          Tim Daly and Lysette Anthony
          Dr. Jekyll and Ms. Hyde (1995)

"Your sister sucks rhinocerous dicks."
Dan Monahan
Porky's II: The Next Day (1983)

"The American public's attention span
is about as long as your dick!"

G. D. Spradlin
Canadian Bacon (1995)

"Hey, it's not what you know, it's who you blow."

Robert Casardo
Me & Him (1989)

"We have X-rated tapes in case you
   need some help."
"Help? Help? I lettered in this in high
   school. I used to keep a picture of my
   right hand in my wallet!"
   Deb Lucusta and Billy Crystal making a
   donation at a sperm bank
   Forget Paris (1995)

"Melvin, you jerk off so much that if you ever did get laid you'd probably scream out your own name."

Unidentified
Screwballs (1983)

"How many pairs of my socks did you borrow? I can almost see your religion."

Jack Thompson referring to
Russell Crowe's crotch
The Sum of Us (1995)

"You're thinking with your little head.
Think with your big head, please."
Jeremy Piven
Dr. Jekyll and Ms. Hyde (1995)

"Sir, you should really put that case in
the compartment above your head."
"I'll keep it with me."
"I can help you if you can't get it up."
Julie Hagerty and Sonny Bono
Airplane II—The Sequel (1982)

"Now call me a prude if you want, but I don't think it's good policy for the Navy to hand over a billion-dollar piece of equipment to a man who has 'Welcome Aboard' tatooed on his penis!"

Bruce Dern
Down Periscope (1996)

"Hey, who do I have to blow to get a
cup of coffee around here?"

Bash Halow
Lie Down With Dogs (1994)

"Jesus, what do I have to do to get my
dick sucked these days?"

Michael Imperioli
Postcards From America (1995)

"Did you hear about the Polack bank
robber? He tied up the safe and blew
the guard."

Unidentified
Flashdance (1983)

"I've got to see a man about a penguin."
Bob Hope
My Favorite Blonde (1942)

"Puberty is over—onwards and upwards!"

Jonathan Silverman
Brighton Beach Memoirs (1986)

"You wouldn't know reality if it was
stuck up your ass."

Raul Julia
Kiss of the Spider Woman (1985)

"You cocksucker."
"Not me, Chief. I'm not the one on my
   knees."

Unidentified and Charles Durning
The Choirboys (1978)

"The penis astonishes me. It can give
pain and pleasure. It can give life,
and now it can give death."
"Pesky little devils, aren't they?"
Unidentified and Kathy Kinney
Parting Glances (1986)

"Big things may happen to that little
thing of yours."
Al Pacino to Chris O'Donnell
Scent of a Woman (1992)

"I hate fattening things. That is why I
do not like oral sex."

Moon Zappa
Little Sister (1991)

"Only yesterday it was *Big Bird*—and today, *You and Your Penile Implant*."
Michele Lane commenting on Shelley Long's selection of videos
Frozen Assets (1992)

"Shake your lizard, let it drain,
    move your hips and spell your name,
    send it straight and send it hard,
    now a sword fight, go *'en garde.'*
    Eat your veggies, eat your starches,
    lean back boys—golden arches."

Daniel Stern
to a group of peeing boy scouts
Bushwacked (1995)

"You know, he reminds me of you."
"Yeah, he is pretty well hung, at that."
Bruce Willis to Paul Newman,
referring to his Doberman
Nobody's Fool (1994)

"What are you doing here?"
"I'm watching you be a prick."
"Well, you ain't seen nothin' yet."
Alan Rachins and Elizabeth Berkley
Showgirls (1995)

"With a name like Big, you're either
seven feet tall, you're a midget or
you got a microscopic wee wee."
Darryl Sivad talking to "Tiny" Lister Jr.
on the telephone
Talkin' Dirty After Dark (1991)

"Why should I pay you more than Steve
was getting?"
"Steve didn't give you a hard-on."
Tony Roberts and Ellen Barkin
Switch (1991)

"What is an aphrodisiac?"
"The word comes from the African root
  'aphro,' meaning *large penis* and the
  greek 'disiac,' which means '*want
  it bad.*'"

Matthew Causey and Frank Galati
The Party Animal (1983)

"This gives me a hard-on."
"Don't tease me."

Barry Tubb and Whip Hubley
Top Gun (1986)

"Did you bump uglies with my sister?"
Sylvester Stallone
Tango & Cash (1989)

"This one is different, she thinks we're
   in love."
"In love with you? Then I have the
   penis of a dromedary."
"Well then, listen carefully camel dick!"
   Bart Braverman and Phil Dishkin
   Hollywood Hot Tubs 2 (1990)

"Jeeze, are you sure?"
"Does the Trojan horse have a wooden dick?"

Woody Allen and Jack Warden
Mighty Aphrodite (1995)

"He's the top dog, the big man, numero uno honcho—the head cheese."

William Shatner
Airplane II—The Sequel (1982)

"What if the baby can see?"

"See what, my love?"

"Your penis, coming toward it. That could scare the hell out of a baby. ... What if your penis hit it in the head? It could cause brain damage, or something."

A pregnant Julianne Moore explaining why she doesn't want to have sex with Hugh Grant
Nine Months (1995)

"Look at those two. One of these days
their dicks are gonna fall off."
"… Dennis will just use another part of
his body."

Ken Olin and Tony Spiridakis
Queens Logic (1991)

"Maybe we should just grow peckers
and join up."

Elizabeth Perkins
Sweet Hearts Dance (1988)

"Hey, kid, what do you use for a jockstrap? A rubber band and a peanut shell?"

Robert Archambault
Porky's (1981)

"I didn't stuff my pants—God did that."
David Keith
Heartbreak Hotel (1988)

"Something tells me you could really fit into a pair of Jockey shorts."

Tammy Grimes
Can't Stop the Music (1980)

"Now that I see you, let me ask you
   something. Does that come in an
   adult size?"

Whoopi Goldberg
Fatal Beauty (1987)

"Why is it that a woman always thinks the most savage thing she can say to a man is to impugn his cocksmanship?"

William Holden
Network (1976)

"You'll make a lovely bride and I'm sure you'll give my son a big bone-fest of a honeymoon."

Joan Plowright
Mr. Wrong (1996)

"What could he have been thinking of?"
"Probably the same thing he was
thinking with."

Gena Rowlands and Kyra Sedgwick
discussing Dennis Quaid
cheating on his wife.
Something To Talk About (1995)

"Move it, dildo breath."

Kaki Hunter
Porky's II: The Next Day (1983)

"You know what I think? I think you
need a Buzzard sausage sandwich
smothered in underwear."

Stephen Baldwin
whose character name is Buzzard
Under the Hula Moon (1995)

"What's the matter, haven't you ever
seen one of these before?"
"Yeah, but the one I seen was life-size."
William McNamara to Erika Eleniak
standing naked before her.
Girl in the Cadillac (1995)

"It says in the manual …"
"If the manual said to stick your wiener
in a light socket, would you do it?"
Ari Greenberg and Daniel Stern
Bushwacked (1995)

"I figure, in this world, you're either being blown away or you're being blown."

Eric Bogosian
Naked in New York (1994)

"You were just pulling my lariat."
Cleavon Little
Blazing Saddles (1974)

"What if somebody looks under my holster flap and sees I'm not packin' a rod?"

Judge Reinhold
Off Beat (1986)

"I wish I had a cock, so I could do this
to you."

Marcia Gay Harden
Crush (1992)

"You've got the philosophy of a dog—
if you can't fuck it or eat it, then piss
on it."

John Jenkins
Patti Rocks (1988)

"What's a wiener?"
"More trouble than it's worth."

Unidentified drag queen
Vegas in Space (1993)

"Okay wrestlers, we have a big meet tomorrow, so no beatin' the meat tonight."

Unidentified coach
The World According To Garp (1982)

"Why is yours bigger than mine?"
"Genetics, pee wee."
Kurt Russell and Sylvester Stallone
talking about their guns.
Tango & Cash (1989)

"I can't tell you how relieved I was when you took off your dress and you didn't have a dick."

Christian Slater
True Romance (1993)

"Dunlop, you suck cock."
"All I can get."

Paul D'Amato and Paul Newman
Slap Shot (1977)

"It's a boy. ..."
"So that means you presumably can
    actually see his whatnot?"
"Penis."
"And it's fine—size-wise and all that
    kind of stuff?"
"Perfect."

Hugh Grant and Emily Yancy
Nine Months (1995)

"God gave men brains larger than dogs
so they wouldn't hump womens' legs
at cocktail parties."

Angela Jolie
Hackers (1995)

"You know as well as I do that the angle of the dangle, times the heat of the meat, equals the mass of the ass."
"Right."

Brian Kerwin and David Wilson
Hometown U.S.A. (1978)

"If there's ever anything I can do for
    you or—more to the point, to you—
    you let me know, okay?"
"Can you hammer a six-inch spike
    through a board with your penis?"
                    Val Kilmer and Deborah Foreman
                              Real Genius (1985)

"I just wanna die with a big dick in my mouth."

Unidentified man
Postcards From America (1995)

"If I masturbated as much as I wanted to, I swear to God I would live in a constant state of guilt—not to mention hospitalization."

Mike McGlone
The Brothers McMullen (1995)

"Your friend Russell told us plenty."
"Like what?"
"He said your dick was bigger than
    your brain!"
"He said that?"
"I don't think he meant it as a
    compliment."

Nicholas Pasco and Joaquin Phoenix
To Die For (1995)

"You got no confidence. I like that in a man. I can't stand those johns who come in here, throw down a couple a hundred, whip out a big dick and wave it all over the joint."

"Oh, I couldn't do that even if I wanted to."

Mira Sorvino and Woody Allen
Mighty Aphrodite (1995)

"I think I'm gonna cut their peckers off
and put key chains on them."
"Their peckers aren't big enough for
key chains."

Robert Joy and Jerzy Skolimowski
Big Shots (1987)

"It's not who stands behind every man,
it's what stands in front."

Mark Linn-Baker
Me & Him (1989)

"You should know that included with the rent around here is a complimentary blow job."

Elisabeth Shue
Leaving Las Vegas (1995)

"I didn't learn to masturbate until after I had sex."

"Are you kidding? I started when I was four. My babysitter caught me humping my Mother Goose book. I've never found a dick as hard as that book!"

Kim Cattrall and Dana Delany
Live Nude Girls (1995)

"You know I've dreamt a lot about your prick lately."
"Was it nicer in your dreams?"

Jeanne Moreau and Brad Davis
Querelle (1982)

"What's the problem with your
   member?"
"Well, I never thought of him as a
   member. I kinda always thought of
   him as a loner."

Matthew Causey
The Party Animal (1983)

"She was giving me the kind of look I could feel in my hip pocket."

Leslie Nielsen
Naked Gun (1988)

"Don't look now, but I think Paul's
    masturbating."
"Make him stop."
"I can't, he's using my hand."

Unidentified
Screwballs (1983)

"I wouldn't sit here too long. The tip of your
dick will freeze to the top of the step. Oh,
I forgot, yours ain't that long."
"Yours ain't either."
"'Cause I fold it."

Paul Newman and Pruitt Taylor Vince
Nobody's Fool (1994)

"Don't be so hard on yourself, Clarence.
It's not your fault that your brain's
the same size as your dick!"

Adam Beach
Dance Me Outside (1994)

"Polishing the old torpedo, sir?"
Rob Schneider to Kelsey Grammer
Down Periscope (1996)

"I'm gonna spank that monkey!"
Matt LeBlanc
Ed (1996)

"I'm Valentine, and I've got a heart-on for you."

Sara Ballantine
Frozen Assets (1992)

"Ted, Ted, Simon just ejected. ..."
"Simon was a fool to eject now."
"You mean?"
"That's right, premature ejection."
Julie Hagerty and Robert Hays
Airplane II—The Sequel (1982)

"You're so ugly, I wouldn't fuck you
with his dick!"

Chris Mulkey
Patti Rocks (1988)

"What do dildos and soy beans have in
   common?"
"What?"
"They're both meat substitutes."
>> *Eric Roberts and Margaret Cho*
>> *It's My Party* (1995)

"It's a liberal thing. One day you're saving the rain forest, the next you're chugging cock!"

Christopher Walken
Things To Do in Denver When You're Dead
(1996)

"The fellas in our family only have to
    look at a woman and she's pregnant."
"It must be because you're all cock-
    eyed."

Malcolm Douglas and Julie Walters
Educating Rita (1983)

"I couldn't get it up right now if you were a pair of twins in a vat of Mazola oil!"

Patrick Swayze
Grandview, U.S.A. (1984)

"Is that a test tube in my pocket, or am I
just happy to see you?"

Eddie Murphy
The Nutty Professor (1996)

"I'll tell you what. Why don't the two of us sit down, have a little drink and discuss this? You look like you could use a stiff one."

Jeremy Piven
Dr. Jekyll and Ms. Hyde (1995)

"I don't want to say anything negative about your penis, but I just can't imagine putting it in my mouth."

Victor Ertmanis
Paris, France (1993)

"Hey Jack, ever get a boner? You know, an erector?"

"Not yet. I'm hoping to get one for Christmas."

Mario Yedidia and Robin Williams
Jack (1996)

"Being up in the sticks, man, you must
   lose your mind around here with
   nothin' to do. Wack off a lot?"
"What's a lot?"
   Adam Sandler and Mark Roberts
   Bulletproof (1996)

"There hasn't been a year like this since Benny Berman laid his dick out on the overhead projector in old man Wiseman's class."

Max Perlich
Plain Clothes (1988)

"Would you like to sleep with me?"
"I'm not sleeping with you."
"I suppose a blow job's out of the
    question?"

> *James Belushi and JoBeth Williams*
> *Parallel Lives* (1995)

"In real life, the chief is the one with the biggest weenie!"

Jacques Dufilho
War of the Buttons (1962)

"People here go through jobs like condoms."

Bash Halow
Lie Down With Dogs (1994)

"I certainly hope you learned a valuable lesson."

"Oh yes. Basically as far as vasectomies go, never use the home kit."

Jon Lovitz
and a pregnant Natasha Gregson Wagner
High School High (1996)

"I don't want to hear any more about penises!"

Rosanna Arquette to her children
who are discussing the size of
Jean-Claude Van Damme's penis
Nowhere To Run (1993)

ABOUT THE AUTHOR

Author and self-described film fanatic, Steve Stewart writes about sexuality in the movies—especially about sexual taboos. In the past decade he has written several movie books including *Full-Frontal Male Nudity Video Guide* (currently on a number of best-seller book lists), *The Voyeur Video Guide to Special-Interest Male Erotic Videos, Gay Hollywood Film & Video Guide* and *Campy, Vampy, Trampy Movie Quotes*.